Lighthouses of the Carolinas for Kids

Terrance Zepke

Pineapple Press, Inc.
Sarasota, Florida

Inquiries should be addressed to:

Pineapple Press, Inc.
P.O. Box 3889
Sarasota, Florida 34230
www.pineapplepress.com

Library of Congress Cataloging-in-Publication Data

Zepke, Terrance
  Lighthouses of the Carolinas for kids / Terrance Zepke.
      p. cm.
  Includes index.
  ISBN 978-1-56164-429-2 (pbk. : alk. paper)
  1. Lighthouses--North Carolina--Juvenile literature. 2.
Lighthouses--South Carolina--Juvenile literature. I. Title.
  VK1024.N8Z47 2008
  387.1'5509756--dc22

                              2008020456

First Edition
10 9 8 7 6 5 4 3 2 1

Design by Shé Hicks
Printed in China

CONTENTS

Part I

All About Lighthouses

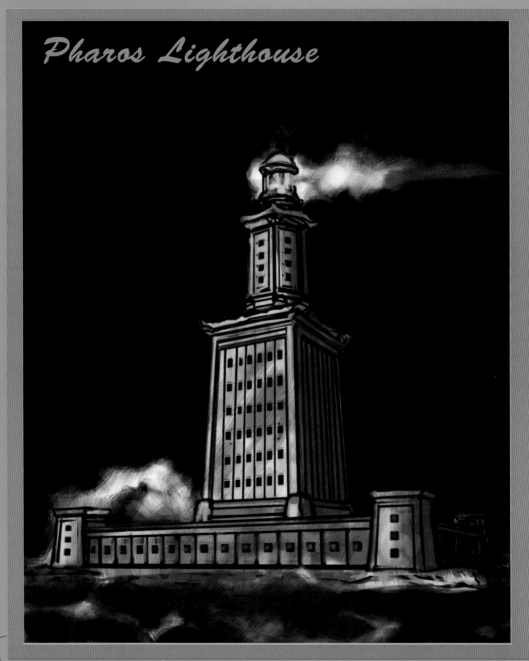

Pharos Lighthouse

History of Lighthouses

Do you know why lighthouses were so important? Do you know how they work? A lighthouse is a tower with a light at the top. This is called the lantern. Lighthouses are navigational aids. They help ships know where they are and where to go. Think of them as road signs for boats and ships. Most importantly, lighthouses keep ships away from dangerous areas. Anywhere that the water is shallower than it seems can be dangerous. Any water that has shoals (shallow areas) is dangerous. The ships can get stuck on the shoals. Then the ship becomes damaged when it tries to get off the shoal. This can make it sink.

Lighthouses have been around for a very long time. Before they existed, it was hard to travel by boat at night. People on shore had to build big fires. The fires showed the ships the way home. Later, fire baskets replaced fires. Long poles with baskets on top were put in the ground. A fire was lit inside these metal baskets. Fire baskets on poles were better because they were easier to see. It was also easier to keep the fire lit inside a basket because it wasn't exposed to wind or rain.

The first lighthouse was built in 280 B.C. in Alexandria, Egypt. It was named **Pharos Lighthouse** because it was on the island of Pharos. This lighthouse was one of the Seven Wonders of the Ancient World. At 450 feet high, it is still one of the tallest lighthouses in the world. That's as high as a forty-five-story skyscraper! Men built this lighthouse by hand. There were no machines to do the work back then. That's why it took twenty years to finish the project. It stood for nearly 1,500 years before an earthquake destroyed it. This was long before electricity was invented. Its light came from a huge fire built inside a room at the top of the tower. Slaves, supervised by priests, kept the light burning every night.

Our first lighthouse was built more than two hundred years after America was discovered. By the end of the American Revolutionary War in 1783, there were twelve lighthouses in America. The first American lighthouse was **Boston Light** on Little Brewster Island. It was built in Boston, Massachusetts, in 1716. It is also known as the Boston Harbor Light Station. The forty-foot-tall tower was destroyed during the Revolutionary War. Another was built there in 1783. The light was automated in 1998. This was the last U.S. lighthouse to be automated. Even though it is automated, Boston Light still has lighthouse keepers. Visitors like to see lighthouse keepers!

Boston
Light

What Is Going on with Lighthouses Today?

The Coast Guard became responsible for America's lighthouses in 1939. When automated lighting systems were put in, keepers were no longer needed. There are now new ways for ships to detect problems, such as radar and sonar. This means that most lighthouses are no longer needed. The Coast Guard works with local groups to protect our lighthouses because of their historical value.

Building Lighthouses

Lighthouses come in all different sizes and shapes. They can be short or tall. It depends on where they're located. A taller lighthouse is needed on flat land. A shorter one will work at the top of a cliff. They can be round, square, multisided, or an open framework style. Sometimes a house for the keeper was combined with the lighthouse. This was a house with a lantern room on top of the roof. Most lighthouses were built on land. Others were built out in the water.

Sullivan's Island Lighthouse in South Carolina (see page 49) is an exception to normal lighthouse design. It is unusual because it is one of the last lighthouses built in the United States. By that time engineers had learned that a three-sided lighthouse would withstand a hurricane better.

Another unusual lighthouse design is called a "Texas tower." These lighthouses got their name because they look like the giant steel structures used in offshore oil drilling in Texas. Only six were ever built. Two are in North Carolina. They are Diamond Shoals Light Tower (see page 36) and Frying Pan Shoals Light Tower (see page 37).

Many different materials were used to build lighthouses. It depended on the design and what was available. These materials include stone, concrete, wood, brick, steel, cast iron, metal, and tabby (a mixture of shells, lime, sand, and water).

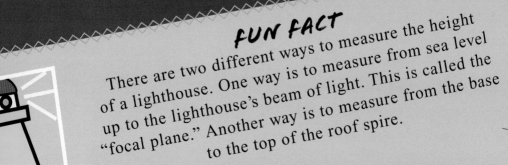

FUN FACT

There are two different ways to measure the height of a lighthouse. One way is to measure from sea level up to the lighthouse's beam of light. This is called the "focal plane." Another way is to measure from the base to the top of the roof spire.

Life of a Lighthouse Keeper

What do you think life was like for a lighthouse keeper? Lazy days spent swimming and napping? Nights spent counting the stars?

No way! This was a hard job. Before electricity was invented, keepers had to climb up to the lantern room each evening and light the lamp. They had to return at sunrise to put out the light. The keeper and his assistants usually worked eight-hour shifts. Some lighthouses had only one keeper. The keeper worked longer hours if he didn't have any assistants. During the night, the keeper climbed the steps up to the lantern room as many as four times. He had to make sure the light was working properly. He had to carry gallons of oil up to the lantern room to fuel the light. He had to wind the clockwork regularly so that the light kept working correctly. He also had to keep a record of all passing ships.

Keepers were called "wickies" because they had to trim the lamp wick. It had to be trimmed daily so that it burned brightly. Keepers had to clean the windows every day. They also polished the lamps. There many other chores that had to be done. These included painting and making repairs. The Lighthouse Board inspected the lighthouses every few months. To pass inspection, everything from the lighting system to the privy (bathroom) had to be in top condition. This was a very important job. Lighthouse keepers were personally hired by the President of the United States. A keeper had to be able to read and write. He had to be in good enough health to be able to do whatever manual labor might be needed. No one under the age of eighteen or over fifty was hired. There was a three-month probation period. This meant that you had to prove you could do the job. Keepers could be removed and sent to another lighthouse. They were expected to move if they were needed somewhere else.

Even with all these duties, keepers were not paid much. Most keepers raised livestock and caught fish to help feed their families. Some took second jobs for extra money. They weren't supposed to do this and could get in trouble if they got caught. Because lighthouses were often located at remote places, hard work was a good thing. It kept the keepers from getting too bored or lonely.

Depending on the lighthouse, it could take up to five keepers to work the light station. Ever since 1883, lighthouse keepers have had to wear uniforms. The dress uniform was dark blue pants, vest, coat, and cap. There was a brown suit that was supposed to be worn when doing outside chores. They wore a uniform apron over the dress uniform when cleaning inside the lighthouse.

Entries from a keeper's journal show
how boring this life can be.

January 11 - One barge passed at 8 p.m.
January 12 - Day of rest.
January 13 - Fixed and painted tank in storage shed.
January 14 - Filled and trimmed lamps.

Even our government realized how boring a keeper's life could be! By the late 1800s, reading materials were given to lighthouse keepers. The government was worried that if keepers got too bored, they might take up other activities or a second job. These things might keep them from doing a good job.

The first lighthouse keeper was George Worthylake at Boston Light. He made $250 a year. This was a lower middle-class wage. Most keepers made from $100 to $600 a year. It depended on whether they were the keeper or an assistant. The pay was also based on where they were stationed. Keeper Worthylake and his family drowned in 1718 when their boat capsized on their way back to the lighthouse. They had gone to town for the day.

There have been eighty female keepers. Most hadn't been hired. They took over the job when a father or husband became ill or died. Two of the most famous were Abbie Burgess and Ida Lewis. Both women served nearly forty years. Abbie also took care of her entire family. Ida rescued eighteen people during her years as keeper. Some women became unofficial keepers. They had to take care of the lighthouse while their husbands took second jobs to support the family. Extra money could be made fishing, whaling, or being a lightering pilot.

Ladies of the Light

At age fourteen **Abbie Burgess** moved to Matinicus Rock Light in Maine with her family. Matinicus Rock is four miles from shore. During the winter of 1856, her father had to go by boat to get supplies. He was unable to get back for a month due to a big storm. Abbie took care of the lighthouse all by herself. She also took care of her four younger sisters and sickly mother. Abbie moved the family out of the keeper's house into the lighthouse. She thought it would be safer, and she was right. The storm swept their house out to sea! When a new keeper was appointed, Abbie stayed on as assistant. She earned $440 a year. She later moved to another lighthouse in Maine where she became the keeper after her husband died.

Ida Lewis also helped her father. He was the keeper at Lime Rock Lighthouse in Rhode Island. He got sick and wasn't able to do the job. Ida took over. She also took care of her sick father and the rest of the family. She rowed the boat over to the mainland and back every. It was the only way her siblings could go to school. When her father died, Ida became the official lighthouse keeper. She was paid $500 a year. In 1924 Lime Rock Lighthouse was renamed the Ida Lewis Lighthouse. This is the only lighthouse renamed in honor of a keeper.

Busy keepers get a little rest in the original Cape Hatteras Lighthouse keeper's house.

Lighthouse Keeper Rules

By 1896, all keepers were civil servants. This meant they worked for the government. The federal government issued these rules for all U.S. lighthouse keepers to follow:

1. You are to light the lamps every evening at sun-setting, and keep them continually burning, bright and clear, till sun-rising.

2. You are to be careful that the lamps, reflectors, and lanterns, are constantly kept clean, and in order; and particularly to be careful that no lamps, wood, or candles, be left burning any where as to endanger fire.

3. In order to maintain the greatest degree of light during the night, the wicks are to be trimmed every four hours, taking care that they are exactly even on the top.

4. You are to keep an exact amount of the quantity of oil received from time to time; the number of gallons, quarts, gills, &c., consumed each night; and deliver a copy of the same to the Superintendent every three months, ending 31 March, 30 June, 30 September, and 31 December, in each year; with an account of the quantity on hand at the time.

5. You are not to sell, or permit to be sold, any spirituous liquors on the premises of the United States; but will treat with civility and attention, such strangers as may visit the Light-house under your charge, and as may conduct themselves in an orderly manner.

6. You will receive no tube-glasses, wicks, or any other article which the contractors, Messr. Morgan & Co., at New Bedford, are bound to supply, which shall not be of suitable kind; and if the oil they supply, should, on trial, prove bad, you will immediately acquaint the Superintendent therewith, in order that he may exact from them a compliance with this contract.

7. Should the contractors omit to supply the quantity of oil, wicks, tube-glasses, or other articles necessary to keep the lights in continual operation, you will give the Superintendent timely notice thereof, that he may inform the contractors and direct them to forward the requisite supplies.

8. You will not absent yourself from the Light-house at any time, without first obtaining the consent of the Superintendent, unless the occasion be so sudden and urgent as not to admit of an application to that officer; in which case, by leaving a suitable substitute, you may be absent for twenty-four hours.

9. All your communications intended for this office must be transmitted through the Superintendent, through whom the proper answer will be returned.

Lighting a Lighthouse

Over the years, there have been many sources used to light the lamps. These include whale oil (made from whale fat), Coiza oil (made from cabbages), lard oil (made from animal fat), kerosene, and finally, electricity (beginning in 1879).

Before oil or electricity, fire and candles were used. Eddystone Lighthouse in England used as many as sixty candles to light it.

The lighting systems also changed a lot over the years. By the mid-1800s, all of our lighthouses used Fresnel lenses.

The Fresnel (pronounced "freh-NELL") lens was one of the greatest lighting discoveries. The lens is named after its French inventor, Augustin-Jean Fresnel. He learned that by placing prisms (glass pieces) in a certain pattern around the oil lamps, the light power increased greatly. The prisms were held in place by a brass framework on a pedestal.

There are many sizes of Fresnel lenses, called "orders." The largest is a first order. Fourth- through sixth-order lenses were used for inland or harbor lights. First through third were used for seacoast lights. Cape Hatteras (page 23) was a seacoast light so it needed the brightest light—a first-order Fresnel lens. On the other hand, Georgetown Lighthouse (page 40) was an inland light. This meant that it needed only a fourth-order Fresnel lens. This was later replaced with a fifth-order lens.

The light could be fixed or flashing. Fixed meant it was steady and did not blink. Flashing meant it blinked. To make the light flash, there were gears that turned the light. Over the years, there have been lots of advancements to the framework and gear system. But the light still works using the same principle from the 1800s.

Many of the lighthouses no longer have their Fresnel lenses. They were removed when the lighthouses were decommissioned. That means they were deactivated or taken out of service.

Lighthouse Terms

AEROBEACON: modern light used in many lighthouses. (See Revolving Light.)

ARGAND LAMP: hollow wick oil lamp.

AUTOMATED: when a light no longer has to be manually turned on and off but is controlled by a computer or timer (or similar system).

CANDLEPOWER: the measurement of how strong a light is, how far away it can be seen. One candlepower equals the light of one candle.

CAPE: a piece of land that extends out into the water. If boats and ships don't know where a cape is, they might hit it. We have many capes in the Carolinas, such as Cape Hatteras and Cape Romain.

CHANNEL: the bed of a stream or river. It is the deep part of a river or harbor.

DAYMARK: color of paint and pattern on a lighthouse that makes it easy to tell which lighthouse it is during the day.

EROSION: when water carries sand away from the beach or an island. This can cause the island or beach to erode or disappear over time.

FIXED LIGHT: steady, nonflashing beam.

FOG SIGNAL: a whistle, bell, horn, or siren that is sounded when there is heavy fog so ships won't run aground on a shoal.

FRESNEL LENS: prisms (glass pieces) that have been cut and fitted around the lamp bulb. Hundreds of prisms are needed to cover the bulb. Because of the design, the light from the lamp bulb refracts or bends as it passes through these prisms in such as way as to produce a single strong beam of light.

GALLERY: the platform or walkway or balcony found outside the watch room and lantern room. Keepers used the gallery to clean the outside windows of the lantern room.

INLET: a narrow waterway that leads inland from the ocean. A stream or a bay is an inlet. They are usually narrow passages of water between two islands. Boats or ships need a lighthouse to show them the way in the dark.

KEEPER: the person responsible for the lighthouse; the main duty was to light the lighthouse every night and put it out every morning, but there were many other duties.

LAMP: lighting system inside a lens.

LANTERN ROOM: the glass-enclosed room found at the top of the lighthouse that holds the lighting system

LENS: curved piece of glass placed around the light to focus and concentrate it.

LIGHTSHIP: A lightship is basically a lighthouse on a ship. These were used in places where lighthouses could not or should not be built.

LOG: a journal in which keepers recorded daily activities and how much fuel was used.

PARABOLIC: metal bowl-like piece (reflector) with a lamp inside the middle of this reflector.

PRISM: specially cut piece of glass that reflects or refracts light.

RANGE LIGHTS: two light towers that were used to mark the entrance to an inlet or channel. One light was moveable so that it could always line up with the light on the other side of the waterway. The channel or inlet might shift so the light had to shift too! This showed ships or boats exactly what route to take.

REFLECT: to throw or bend back light from a surface.

REFRACT: to deflect or bend light from a surface.

REVOLVING LIGHT: flashing light; with a Fresnel lens, the light doesn't revolve to make it flash but the lens revolves to create a flashing light. An aerobeacon is a flashing light that works differently from a Fresnel lens. Each lighthouse has a different pattern of flashing light to make the light identifiable at night. If you see a certain flashing pattern you can recognize it as being a certain lighthouse, thereby knowing exactly where you are.

SHOAL: a sandy elevation in shallow water caused by waves or currents.

SPIDER LAMP: shallow brass pan filled with oil and several wicks. The wicks are lit just like a candle is lit.

WATCH ROOM: room below the lantern room where the keeper stored fuel and stood watch. The lantern room is too crowded with lighting equipment to stay in for any period of time—and too hot!

WICK HOLLOW: concentric cotton wick used in Argand lamps (and some other lamps).

"WICKIE": nickname given to lighthouse keepers because they spent so much time cleaning and trimming the lamp wicks.

Part II
North Carolina Lighthouses

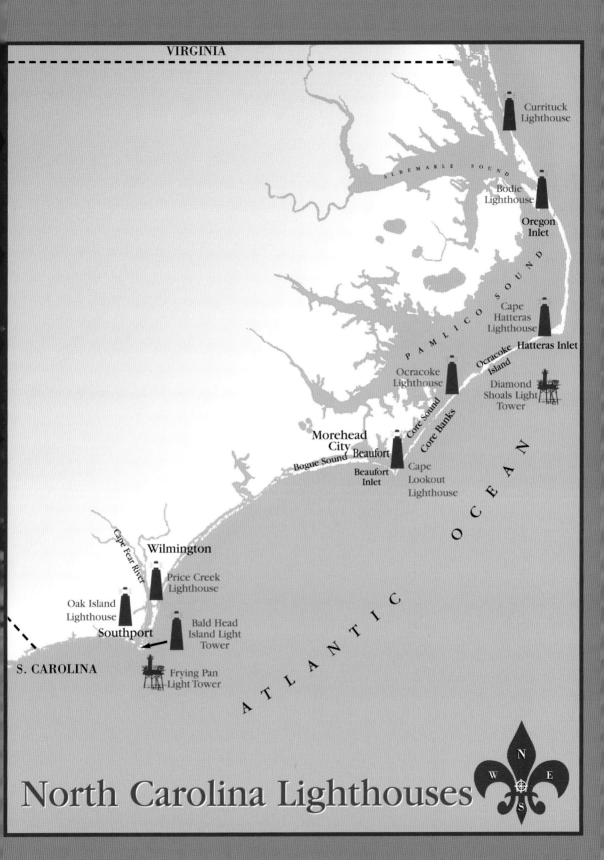

VIRGINIA

Currituck
Lighthouse

ALBEMARLE SOUND

Bodie
Lighthouse

Oregon
Inlet

PAMLICO SOUND

Cape
Hatteras
Lighthouse

Ocracoke
Island Hatteras Inlet

Ocracoke
Lighthouse

Diamond
Shoals Light
Tower

Core Sound

Core Banks

Morehead
City Beaufort

Bogue Sound

Beaufort
Inlet

Cape
Lookout
Lighthouse

OCEAN

Cape Fear River

Wilmington

Price Creek
Lighthouse

ATLANTIC

Oak Island
Lighthouse

Southport

Bald Head
Island Light
Tower

S. CAROLINA

Frying Pan
Light Tower

ATLANTIC

North Carolina Lighthouses

N
W E
S

Currituck Lighthouse

Currituck Lighthouse as it looks today.

Currituck is the farthest north of the four Outer Banks lighthouses of North Carolina. It was the last one built. The plan to build Currituck Lighthouse was approved in the 1860s. The lighthouse wasn't finished and lit until 1875 because of the Civil War.

Currituck Sound was (and is) very shallow, so the big ships that brought in the building supplies had to anchor as far as eight miles out in the ocean. Small boats brought supplies the rest of the way. At the dock the supplies were put in a cart. The cart rolled across tracks built from the dock to the lighthouse site.

It took nearly one million red bricks to build the 162-foot-tall lighthouse. The base is made of stone. Below that a wood foundation goes seven feet below ground. At the widest part of the lighthouse the walls are five feet eight inches thick.

The four Outer Banks lighthouses look very much alike. They are painted with different patterns so ships can tell them apart. Cape Hatteras Lighthouse is painted with black and white vertical stripes, called "candystriping." Bodie Island Lighthouse has horizontal stripes. Cape Lookout Lighthouse has a checkered pattern. Currituck Lighthouse was not painted. Not painting this lighthouse made it different from the other lighthouses and also saved money.

At first, the lighthouse was lit with a mineral oil lamp. It had five large wicks in the center. The white light was "fixed." That means it did not flash. There was also a red light that flashed every ninety seconds. The flash lasted for five seconds. The lighthouse keeper was responsible for hand-cranking the weights. The weights caused the lights to turn or rotate every two and a half hours. During World War I the light had to work twenty-four hours

- Currituck Lighthouse was the last lighthouse built on the Outer Banks. It is the only one that is not painted.
- The brick lighthouse cost $178,000 to build.
- It stands 162 feet tall. There are 214 steps to the top of the lighthouse.

a day. Three keepers worked eight-hour shifts. That way someone was always watching for enemy ships and submarines.

This lighthouse still shines. The light was automated in 1939, so keepers are no longer needed. The light is now electric and flashes in a pattern of three seconds on and seventeen seconds off. Ships can see it up to nineteen miles out to sea. Visitors can explore the inside of the lighthouse, except for the lantern room. There are also two keepers' houses. The smaller one is a museum shop filled with lighthouse souvenirs. The larger house is not open to the public.

The Port O'Plymouth Museum (in Plymouth, North Carolina) maintains a reproduction of an 1886 Roanoke River Lighthouse. There were three Roanoke River lights. Two were in Plymouth and one in Edenton. The one in Edenton has recently been saved by the town. This light is the last surviving river light out of twenty river lights once found along North Carolina's inland waterways.

Close to the Currituck Lighthouse is the historic Whalehead Club. This is a twenty-thousand-square-foot mansion. It is the largest house on the Outer Banks. It was built in 1925 by Edward Collins Knight when his wife was refused admission to the local all-male hunting club. The large home has an elevator and both fresh and salt water for bathing. Whalehead Club is open to the public.

The lighthouse keepers and their families posing for a photograph at Currituck Lighthouse, about 1889.

Bodie Island Lighthouse

Bodie Island Lighthouse, oil shed, and keeper's house.

This brick lighthouse is 170 feet high. It has a day pattern of black-and-white painted bands. This is the third Bodie Island Lighthouse. The first lighthouse was too short and did not have the right lighting system. The second lighthouse was blown up during the Civil War. The remains of the first two lighthouses washed away long ago. The lighthouse you see today is half a mile from the ocean, just north of Oregon Inlet.

This lighthouse was built in 1872. The federal government paid $140,000 to build a lighthouse, keepers' houses, and several outbuildings. The man who was in charge of building Cape Hatteras Lighthouse worked on Bodie Island Lighthouse. For the foundation, he "stacked" timber pilings below the ground. Then he placed granite blocks above the base. This was done so the lighthouse could survive strong winds and storms.

The keeper had to carry kerosene oil to the lantern room every

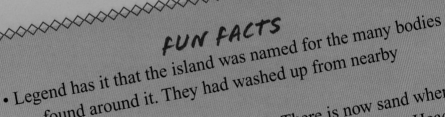

FUN FACTS

- Legend has it that the island was named for the many bodies found around it. They had washed up from nearby shipwrecks.
- Bodie Island is no longer an island. There is now sand where there used to be water. This beach now joins Nags Head Beach.
- The first keeper of Bodie Island Lighthouse was paid $400 a year.

day. He brought it from the oil shed in a large bucket. The lamp was filled with this oil. Then the wick was lit, just like you light a candle. Electricity replaced oil in the early 1930s, so the light changed from fixed to flashing. This means it didn't flash or blink before, but now it does. In the 1950s, the lighting system was changed to an automated 160,000-candlepower beam. Automated means that it works all by itself. No keeper is needed to turn the lights on or off. The lighthouse now has a first-order Fresnel lens. The light can be seen nineteen miles away. It flashes nightly even though it is no longer needed. No one likes to see a dark lighthouse!

There are 214 stairs in Bodie Island Lighthouse. The lighthouse keeper used to climb them several times a day!

Another Type of Light

The Wright brothers flew the first airplane at Kitty Hawk on December 17, 1903. This made North Carolina the "First in Flight" state. This monument was built in 1932. The light on top of the sixty-one-foot-high monument can be seen six miles away.

Cape Hatteras Lighthouse

Cape Hatteras Lighthouse as it appears today.

The first lighthouse at Cape Hatteras was built in 1803. That light did not shine bright enough or far enough. To fix these problems, more height was added to the tower. A brighter light was also installed.

Even with the new first-order Fresnel lens, the small lighthouse wasn't good enough. A taller lighthouse was needed. A new lighthouse was built. It was 197 feet tall. The first-order Fresnel lens was transferred to the new lighthouse. The old lighthouse was torn down when the new one was lit on December 18, 1870.

It looks like a giant, black and white candy cane. Lighthouses were needed during the day and at night. At night, ships could tell them apart by the way the light flashed. That's how they knew where they were. But lighthouses had to be easy to identify during the day too. That way ships knew where they were as soon as they spotted the lighthouse.

By the 1920s, erosion had become a problem. Erosion is when water carries sand away from a beach or island. This can cause an

Moving the Lighthouse

Cape Hatteras Lighthouse had to be moved to protect it from hurricanes. It took months to move the lighthouse to its new home. It is now safely on the other side of the highway. This lighthouse has survived at least one earthquake, more than forty hurricanes, the Civil War, and a major move!

"Cap'n" Unaka Jennette was the keeper at Cape Hatteras Lighthouse from 1919 to 1939. He was the last keeper at this lighthouse. He and his wife, "Miss Sudie," had seven children: Almy, Vivian, Myrtle, Rany, Olive, Dorcas, and Ramona. They were all born in the keeper's house except Almy and Vivian. They had a good childhood. They played with each other and with the assistant keepers' children. All the kids had chores to do. They took care of the livestock and vegetable garden. They went to school. They fished a lot. The family often had yummy fresh seafood for dinner. Movies were shown at the schoolhouse once a week. When Rany Jennette grew up, he became a park ranger at Cape Hatteras National Seashore. He even got married at the lighthouse!

island or beach to erode or disappear over time.

Another lighthouse, made mostly of steel, was built one mile inland. On May 15, 1936, the keeper, Unaka B. Jennette, shut down the big Cape Hatteras light and moved to the new light farther inland. Twelve years later, in 1948, the steel lighthouse was shut down. The old Cape Hatteras Lighthouse was relit. It turned out that it was a better lighthouse. Also, the erosion problem had been taken care of. The old steel beacon was torn down.

By the 1970s, erosion had become a problem again. The lighthouse needed to be moved farther inland if it was going to survive. It took a year to get the beacon ready for its big move. It took $10 million dollars and twelve months to move the lighthouse 1,600 feet away from the shoreline. There have been other lighthouses relocated but none as big as Cape Hatteras. Luckily, there were no problems. This historic lighthouse still shines brightly every night.

The Cape Hatteras Lighthouse is a National Historic Landmark, a National Historic Civil Engineering Landmark, and is on the National Register of Historic Places.

What's a Shoal?

A shoal is a big bed of sand that is found in shallow water (also called a sandbar). A shoal forms when cold and warm water currents collide. If a ship doesn't know the shoal is there, it can get stuck on it and sink. A lighthouse is the best way to warn ships where these shoals are located. Diamond Shoals lie off Cape Hatteras. They are very dangerous because they are more than twelve miles long. This is why Cape Hatteras Lighthouse is so important. So many ships have been lost off Cape Hatteras that it is known as "the graveyard of the Atlantic."

LIFE-SAVING STATIONS WERE AS IMPORTANT AS LIGHTHOUSES.

Chicamacomico Life-Saving Station on Hatteras Island was established in 1874. This was among the first of many lifesaving stations on the Outer Banks. These stations were important because ships often got stuck on shallow shoals and their crews needed rescuing. It was a dangerous job. Chicamacomico is considered to be one of the most complete U.S. Life-Saving Service/Coast Guard Station complexes on the east coast. In the 1940s, Chicamacomico had an honorary surfdog. He was a black Labrador retriever named Fondie. He went with the men on many rescue missions. The dog stood at attention with front paws in the air every time the flag was raised.

The first all–African-American lifesaving crew in the United States was at **Pea Island Life-Saving Station**. This station was built on the Outer Banks in the late 1800s. Richard Etheridge was the first African-American station keeper employed by the Life-Saving Service in 1880. A museum there now honors the brave men who served here from 1880 to 1947.

Cape Hatteras Lighthouse

Cape Hatteras Life-Saving Station. There is a surfing dog, but not Fondie.

Ocracoke Lighthouse

Ocracoke Island is a sixteen-mile island that was once used as a hideout for Blackbeard the pirate. It became an official port in 1715. Many local fishermen became "lightering" pilots. Lightering pilots helped ships safely sail past the dangerous Ocracoke Inlet.

As more ships and people came to Ocracoke, it was decided that a lighthouse was needed. Between 1798 and 1803, a wooden lighthouse was built on nearby Shell Island. The Shell Island Beacon was fifty-four feet tall and topped with a huge oil-fueled lamp. The beacon was destroyed in 1818 by lightning. It was not rebuilt because it was decided that the lighthouse should be on Ocracoke Island.

Ocracoke Lighthouse was lit in 1823. It was built by Noah Porter of Massachusetts. The lighthouse cost $11,359.35, including the three-room keeper's house.

This beacon is sixty-five feet tall. It is made of brick covered with plaster. At the base, the walls are five feet thick! The lighthouse became automated in 1946. The fixed white 8,000-candlepower light comes on every evening before dusk. It can be seen from fourteen miles away.

FUN FACTS

- Ocracoke Lighthouse was built in 1823.
- It is the oldest lighthouse still in service in North Carolina.
- There was once an Indian village where the lighthouse was built.

The best way to reach the island is by private boat or by taking one of the state ferries. The ferries depart from Hatteras Island, Cedar Island, and Swan Quarter. The lighthouse is not open to the public. Visitors can walk around the outside of the lighthouse.

Watch Out for Pirates!

Ocracoke was a pirate's haven. It was made famous by Blackbeard. The story goes that Blackbeard joined a group of Jamaica-bound sailors. They were fighting as privateers in Queen Anne's War against France in the early 1700s. A privateer is pretty much a pirate who has been allowed by the British government to attack enemy ships. Privateers shared the plunder with the government, whereas pirates kept their loot.

After the war, Blackbeard turned from privateering to outright piracy. By the time Blackbeard moved to Ocracoke Island in 1718, he was captain of four ships and four hundred pirates.

Virginia Governor Alexander Spotswood did not like Blackbeard and sent the British Navy to capture him. A great battle took place at Ocracoke Inlet on November 22, 1718.

Legend has it that it took five gunshots and twenty stab wounds to kill Blackbeard! Legend also has it that the British Navy took the pirate's head back to Virginia Governor Spotswood to prove he was dead.

Blackbeard is shown here with "smoking pigtails." He supposedly did this to look scary.

Cape Lookout Lighthouse

There were many shipwrecks before Cape Lookout Lighthouse was built. The lighthouse was needed because of the ten-mile sandbar called Lookout Shoals. Without the lighthouse, ships wouldn't know where this dangerous sandbar was.

The first lighthouse at Cape Lookout was built in 1812. By the 1850s it was clear that it was not good enough. Another beacon was built in 1859. It was a round red brick tower with a first-order Fresnel lens. It cost $45,000 to build. This light could be seen from nineteen miles away.

The lighthouse was so good that Cape Hatteras, Bodie, and Currituck Lighthouses were made the same way. The only difference between these lighthouses was how they were painted. Each had a different design so that they could be easily identified. Cape Lookout Lighthouse is painted with a black-and-white diamond-shaped pattern.

In 1914, the light was changed from a fixed light to a flashing light. The light was automated in 1950. The first-order Fresnel lens was removed in 1975. It was replaced with 2,000-watt aero-beams (airport beacons). There is a generator and an automated back-up system inside the beacon. The lighthouse is owned by the National Park Service. To check on the lighting system, employees must climb 197 steps. Visitors may explore the grounds but the beacon is usually not open to the public.

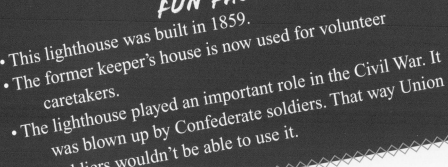
WANNA BE A LIGHTHOUSE KEEPER?

The National Park Service accepts applications for volunteer caretakers. Who can be a volunteer keeper? Anyone who can serve for three months. The job is easy. You greet tourists, answer questions, and keep the house clean. Volunteers stay in the keeper's house. It even has electricity nowadays! There is a waiting list of up to six years for this volunteer job.

Cape Lookout Lighthouse, keepers' houses, and outbuildings in the 1800s. Cape Lookout had two female keepers: Charlotte (1872–1875) and Emily Moore (1876–1878)

CAPE LOOKOUT NATIONAL SEASHORE

The lighthouse is part of Cape Lookout National Seashore. The seashore is made up of fifty-five miles of islands. The biggest part of the seashore is Shackleford Banks and Core Banks. Wild ponies are sometimes seen on Shackleford Banks. These ponies are descendents of Spanish mustangs who survived a shipwreck and have roamed the Banks ever since.

Oak Island Lighthouse

Oak Island Lighthouse was lit on May 15, 1958. This was the last lighthouse built in North Carolina. It is one of the last lighthouses built in America. It is 169 feet high. The black and white paint used to cover the tower was mixed with the concrete. This was done so the lighthouse would never need repainting. The base is anchored seventy feet below ground. The depth of the foundation and the eight-inch-thick concrete used to build the tower help ensure nothing will happen to the lighthouse.

Two Marine Corps helicopters were needed to put the lamp on top of the tower. The lighting system is four 1,000-watt aero-beam lights. The powerful flashing light can be seen twenty-four miles out to sea. Oak Island is one of the most powerful lighthouses in the world. Black panels have been placed over the lantern room windows to prevent "spotlighting" area homes.

Tools, lamps, and other supplies are hauled to the top of the tower using a pulley and metal box. Keepers must climb the small metal steps beside the pulley shaft. At the top of the steps is a ladder that has to be used to access the lantern room. The four revolving lights inside the lantern room are so big that you can't enter the room when the lights are on or you might get hurt.

This was one of the last manually operated lighthouses in the world. Someone had to turn it on each evening from the base of the tower. This was done thirty minutes before sunset. Someone turned it off each morning at thirty minutes past sunrise. The light is now automated. There is even an automatic back-up system. It removes burned-out bulbs and replaces them with new bulbs.

The lighthouse used to be part of the Coast Guard compound. The only way the lighthouse could be seen was from the road, Caswell Beach, or Southport waterfront. The Coast Guard now allows visitors to enter the area around the lighthouse. They cannot go anywhere else in the compound or inside the lighthouse.

This fourteen-rung metal ladder is the only way to get up to the lantern room.

Helicopters placed the lamp on top of the tower.

FUN FACTS

- This lighthouse was built in 1958.
- Oak Island was one of the last lighthouses built in America.
- Paint mixed into the concrete means the lighthouse never has to be repainted.

Oak Island Lighthouse

Price Creek Lighthouse

If you look closely, on the right side of the Price Creek Lighthouse you can see where the bricks were damaged during the Civil War.

Two Price Creek Lighthouses were the last inlet lights to be placed along the Cape Fear River. The two inlet lights were put at both sides of Price Creek in 1849. They were needed to help ships reach the state's biggest port, Wilmington.

One of the Price Creek Lighthouses was destroyed by storms. The other Price Creek Lighthouse still stands. It was damaged during the Civil War. Ships began taking a different route to Wilmington in 1881. This meant the lighthouse was no longer needed. Repairs to the damaged tower were never made. The windows are missing and the lantern room has been removed. Otherwise, Price Creek Lighthouse is in fairly good condition even though it has been abandoned for more than one hundred years.

The lighthouse is owned by a private company that is not interested in saving it. Local groups want to move and repair the old lighthouse but have not raised enough money.

This is a sketch of the other lighthouse that was also at Price Creek but was destroyed by storms.

Bald Head Island Lighthouse

A lighthouse was needed on Bald Head Island to help ships avoid the dangerous sandbars along the Cape Fear River. Frying Pan Shoals is the biggest and worst sandbar. It goes more than twenty miles into the ocean.

Bald Head Island Light Station was North Carolina's first lighthouse. It was lit in 1795. Another lighthouse had to be built in 1817 because of erosion.

The new lighthouse is known as "Old Baldy." At the bottom, it is thirty-six feet wide and its walls are five feet thick. At its top, it is fourteen and a half feet wide and its walls are two feet thick. The foundation is stone. The tower is brick with plaster over it on the outside.

It is 100 feet high and had a fourth-order Fresnel lens. Due to its lack of height and lens, the beacon wasn't good enough. A lightship was put at Frying Pan Shoals to help guide ships from 1854 until 1964. Old Baldy's lens was replaced with a third-order Fresnel lens in 1855. This was a better light. Also, a fog bell was placed near the lighthouse.

The lighthouse was shut down during the Civil War. When Old Baldy was reactivated after the war, the third-order Fresnel lens was replaced with a fourth-order lens. The Lighthouse Board didn't think a sea light was needed anymore. From then on, Old Baldy was nothing more than a harbor light. A 150-foot stone jetty was built to slow erosion. A two-story keeper's house was built in 1883.

Old Baldy was used until 1935. The Fresnel lens was replaced with a radio beacon during World War II. Old Baldy is near the Bald Head Island Marina entrance. The light still comes on nightly. That's because it is a

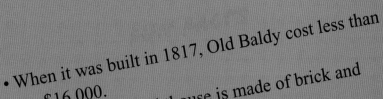

- When it was built in 1817, Old Baldy cost less than $16,000.
- The eight-sided lighthouse is made of brick and coated with cement.
- Bald Head Island Light Station was North Carolina's first lighthouse structure. The 100-foot tower was completed and lit in 1795.

good landmark for ships and a comforting sight for the rest of us. Visitors can climb the 112 wooden steps to the top. No cars are permitted on the island—only bicycles and golf carts can be found.

Captain Sonny Dosher was a longtime keeper at Bald Head. This was the dress uniform worn by a keeper. He wore dark blue pants, a vest, top coat, and hat or cap.

Diamond Shoals Light Tower was a Texas tower. It was almost the same as the Frying Pan Light Tower. Both were destroyed in 2008.

Diamond Shoals Light Tower

This tower was built in 1966 out in the ocean. It is twelve miles from Cape Hatteras. The light flashes white every ten seconds. The huge tower has a galley, eight bedrooms, and a communications center. The Diamond Shoals light can be seen eighteen miles out at sea.

The U.S. Coast Guard is responsible for the tower. The light was automated in 1977. After that the Coast Guard checked on it by helicopter once a year. They didn't need to come more often because there was a back-up lighting system and a signal to notify the Coast Guard of any equipment malfunctions. The lighting system was changed to solar power in 1994. It was seen up to twelve miles away until 2004, when it was deactivated. Its main function after that was as a weather station. Fishermen and forecasters counted on the tower's instruments to report wind and wave conditions. It also served as a daymark or landmark for ships to recognize. Recently, the weather reporting instruments stopped working. They couldn't be repaired because it was too dangerous to land the helicopter on the damaged helicopter landing pad. Diamond Shoals Light Tower was sunk to make an artificial reef in 2007. A weather buoy was placed nearby to give readings for forecasters and fishermen.

What is an artificial reef? Artificial means that it is man-made, rather than made by nature. A natural reef is a strip of rocks, sand, and coral that extends from the bottom of the ocean to near the surface. An artificial reef is a reef that has been created by sinking something like an old ship or lighthouse. Both artificial and natural reefs are good things because they make good breeding grounds for fish. That's why fishing is usually good around a reef!

Frying Pan Light Tower

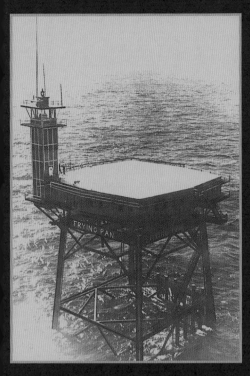

Frying Pan Light Tower was built in 1964–66 to accompany the Oak Island Lighthouse. The tower was needed to replace lightships that had to be removed because of hurricane threats. The tower helped ships get through the dangerous Frying Pan Shoals, which are about thirty miles southeast of Cape Fear. The tower cost $2 million to complete. The "house" or platform was brought by barge all the way from Louisiana. The platform sits on four huge steel posts that are anchored well into the ground below the sea.

The main deck is the crew living space and work area. The lower deck houses the fuel tank and boat. The deck above the main deck is the Helo Deck. This is the helicopter landing pad and recreation area. Tanks that hold fresh water for the station are also on this deck.

The light tower was deactivated in 2004. Light towers were deactivated or shut down when they were no longer needed due to new technology on ships. Like the Diamond Shoals Light Tower, Frying Pan Shoals Light Tower was recently sunk to make an artificial reef.

LIGHTSHIPS

Lightships were used wherever it was impractical to put a lighthouse. These ships had lights at the top of their masts, and sometimes they also had fog bells. The first lightship was used in Chesapeake Bay in 1820. North Carolina had several over the years, including Diamond Shoals Lightship and Frying Pan Shoals Lightship.

South Carolina Lighthouses

Myrtle
Beach

GRAND STRAND

Georgetown
Lighthouse
Georgetown Winyah Bay

FRANCIS

MARION

NATIONAL

FOREST

Cape Romain
Lighthouses

Cape
Romain
Shoals

A T L A N T I C   O C E A N

Sullivan's Island Lighthouse
Charleston

Morris Island
Lighthouse

Beaufort
Hunting
Island
Lighthouse

Hilton Head
Lighthouse
Hilton Head Island
Harbour Town "Lighthouse"
Daufuskie Island
Haig Point Lighthouses

South Carolina Lighthouses

GEORGIA

W N E
S

Georgetown Lighthouse

The Georgetown Lighthouse is on deserted North Island.

Georgetown is the third-oldest port town in South Carolina. At one time it exported more rice than anywhere else in the world. The rice was transported around the world by ships. A lighthouse was needed to help ships get into and out of the harbor.

The Georgetown Lighthouse was lit in 1799. Five years later, the lighthouse was destroyed by a storm.

The lighthouse was rebuilt in 1812. It was made of brick and painted white. During the Civil War, Confederate soldiers used it as an observation tower. Union soldiers took control of the lighthouse in May 1862 until the end of the war.

The lighthouse was badly damaged during the Civil War. It was rebuilt again in 1867. The beacon was made the same way, using brick and then painting it white. This lighthouse

This is how the Georgetown Lighthouse and the former keepers' house once looked.

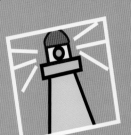
is taller than the first two Georgetown Lighthouses. They were only seventy-two feet tall but this one is eighty-seven feet high. At its widest point, the lighthouse is twenty feet across and its walls are six inches thick. There are 124 stone steps up to the lantern room. A fourth-order Fresnel lens was used when this harbor light was needed.

An oil house, water cistern, and two-story keeper's house were built to go with the lighthouse. There is also an old U.S. Navy radio station and dormitory that was used by the Navy during World War II.

U.S. Coast Guard operated the lighthouse until 1986. That was the year the light was automated. Today it is equipped with a 3500-candlepower light. This light is reflected through a fifth-order Fresnel lens. It can be seen twelve miles away. The light runs day and night because it lacks a timing device to turn it on and off. The U.S. Coast Guard decided it was cheaper to have the light on all the time then it would be to put in a timer. There are two back-up lights powered by battery packs in case a light burns out.

COOL STUFF TO DO

Georgetown Lighthouse is located on North Island. This is a fifteen-mile-long island that is now part of the twenty-thousand-acre Yawkey Wildlife Center. Land has been cleared around the lighthouse. The rest of the island remains wild and overgrown. The wildlife refuge is full of bald eagles, rattlesnakes, loggerhead turtles, exotic birds, and many other animals.

A Ghost Story
The Lighthouse Keeper's Daughter

No one lived on the island where the lighthouse was except for the keeper and his daughter. The keeper sometimes had to row his boat over to Georgetown for food and supplies. He usually took his daughter with him. One day on their way back to the island, a bad storm began. The keeper rowed as hard as he could but the storm kept getting worse. Suddenly, a large wave washed over the boat and knocked the little girl right out of it! The father jumped in the water and swam around trying to find his daughter, but he never did. The little girl had drowned. The keeper was rescued but he never got over the death of his only daughter. The sad man never left the island again. Local fishermen brought him food and supplies. When the lighthouse keeper died, boaters began seeing a man and a little girl rowing around the island. Whenever anyone got close to the boat, it disappeared into thin air! Legend has it that seeing these two ghosts is a warning that a bad storm is coming.

Cape Romain Lighthouses

The two Cape Romain lighthouses. Can you guess which one is leaning?

The government approved a lighthouse to be built on Lighthouse Island in 1823. This seventy-five-acre island was once called Raccoon Key. It is near the entrance to the Santee River. The lighthouse and keeper's house cost $8,425 and were finished in 1827.

A timber piling foundation supports the small lighthouse. The lighthouse is thirty feet across at the bottom and fifteen feet across at the top. The round brick tower was painted black and white.

The light never worked the way it should. In 1847, the old lighting system was replaced. The new system was a fixed light made up of eleven lamps and reflectors. The light was still not good enough. Too many ships wrecked on the nine-mile sandbar called Cape Romain Shoal. Just one year later, it was decided that a better lighthouse was needed. The lighting system was removed and the lighthouse wasn't used anymore. When the new lighthouse was being built, it was discovered that its walls were out of plumb. This means that it wasn't perfectly straight. This happened because the foundation wasn't even. This made the lighthouse lean slightly. The engineer could not fix the problem. The 150-foot lighthouse has always leaned slightly to one side. It has been nicknamed "The Leaning Lighthouse." The lower part of the lighthouse was painted white. There are alternating black and white vertical stripes at the upper part of the tower.

The lantern room contained a first-order Fresnel lens. The light could be seen nineteen miles out to sea. The lighting was replaced in 1931. The new light was a five-hundred-watt bulb inside a turning bull's eye lens. Electricity came from the island's new generating plant. In 1937, the

lighting system was replaced with an automated thousand-candlepower beam.

The first Cape Romain Lighthouse was never destroyed. It was repainted red in 1937. This was so that it wouldn't be confused with the new lighthouse. Only the bottom part of the original lighthouse still exists. The Coast Guard replaced the new lighthouse with lighted buoys in 1947. It was no longer needed. Almost all of the outbuildings were destroyed that same year. The only structure that survived was the keeper's house. It was removed in the 1950s. The generating plant is gone too.

Both lighthouses remain on North Island as daymarkers. Not much remains of the original lighthouse. The second Cape Romain Lighthouse is in pretty good shape. It was weatherproofed a few years ago. A 195-step spiral stairway leads to the lantern room.

FUN FACTS

- The two towers are exceptions to the "twin tower" rule. When a new lighthouse is built, the old lighthouse is supposed to be destroyed. No one knows why, but the old lighthouse was not destroyed when the new one was built.
- The lighthouses are part of the sixty-five-thousand-acre Cape Romain National Wildlife Refuge. About 350 kinds of birds, mammals, reptiles, and amphibians can be found in this refuge.
- Cape Romain was named in honor of St. Romano. This land was discovered by a Spanish explorer on St. Romano's birthday.

Cape Romain Lighthouses

Murder at Cape Romain

One of the former keepers at Cape Romain Lighthouse was a mean man named Fischer. Fischer liked the deserted island and he loved being a lighthouse keeper. His wife did not like living there. Fischer was kept busy with his duties as lighthouse keeper. There wasn't much for his wife to do. She was sad and homesick for their native Norway. All of her family and friends lived in Norway. She begged her husband to let her visit Norway. He refused. The woman finally told her husband that she was going home for a long visit. Fischer was so angry that he killed his wife with a kitchen knife.

The keeper told people that his wife had committed suicide. No one suspected the terrible truth. The lighthouse keeper told what had really happened as he was dying of old age. Legend has it that drops of blood mysteriously appeared on the floor of the keeper's house. The blood was always at the same spot where the woman had been killed. Footsteps were often heard upstairs. Whenever anyone went upstairs to find out who was making the noise, no one was there! The strange noises and drops of blood appeared until the house was finally destroyed.

Sullivan's Island Lighthouse (Charleston Light)

One of the last lighthouses built in America was Sullivan's Island Lighthouse, which is also called Charleston Light by some people. It was lit on June 15, 1962. It is on the north side of the Charleston Harbor. The tower was painted orange and white, but was repainted black and white.

The 140-foot lighthouse is very different from older lighthouses. It is anchored by steel girders. It is three-sided, like a triangle. It is covered in aluminum paneling. All of these things were done to make it hurricane-proof. It also has many things that you won't find in any other lighthouse, such as an elevator. The elevator goes almost all the way to the top of the lighthouse. The only way to enter the lantern room is by using the stairs near the top. Something else that you won't find in other lighthouses are offices. And these offices are air-conditioned!

The original lighting system was very different from what is now being used. There was a 28,000,000-candlepower apparatus! This lighthouse was probably one of the most powerful lights in the world. It was so powerful that it was too much. In 1967, the lighting system was replaced with three low-intensity lamps. This reduced the candlepower to 1,170,000. The lights can still be seen more than twenty-six miles away! The lights were automated in 1982. A back-up system was installed in case lights burned out. This is a good thing since the lights shine day and night. One bulb blinks every five seconds. The second blinks every twenty seconds. The third blinks every thirty seconds.

Sullivan's Island Lighthouse is part of a Coast Guard facility. It is not open to the public. There is an old boathouse, keeper's house, and storage building. They came from South Carolina's only Lifesaving Station. The buildings are used by Coast Guard employees. They are listed on the National Register of Historic Places.

This former keeper's house has been restored and is used for lighthouse personnel.

FUN FACTS

- Sullivan's Island Lighthouse was the last lighthouse to be built in South Carolina.
- It replaced the old Morris Island Lighthouse.
- It is one of the most powerful lights in the world. It is air-conditioned inside and has an elevator.

Sullivan's Island Lighthouse

Morris Island Lighthouse

The Morris Island Lighthouse is six miles southeast of Charleston. Putting a lighthouse here was important because Charleston is South Carolina's biggest port. It is the second lighthouse built here to protect this area.

The original Morris Island Lighthouse was a 102-foot brick tower. The light was fueled by lard oil. The revolving lamp could be seen twelve miles away. The lighthouse was built in 1767. England's King George III approved it because America was still an English colony until after the Revolutionary War. This lighthouse was one of only two lighthouses south of Delaware Bay to survive the war. The other one was Tybee Island Lighthouse in Georgia.

The first shot of the Civil War was fired from Morris Island in 1861. During the Civil War, Confederate soldiers blew up the lighthouse. They did that so that Union soldiers couldn't use it as an observation tower.

In 1873, the government approved another lighthouse. It would replace the one destroyed during the Civil War. It took three years and $150,000 to build the second Morris Island Lighthouse. It stands four hundred yards southeast of the original lighthouse due to the changing channel. It is built on pilings that go fifty feet below ground. The tower is thirty-three feet across at the widest part and nearly seventeen feet across at the top. The 161-foot

- The original Charleston Lighthouse was built by order of King George III of England before the Revolutionary War.
- The lighthouse you see today is the second one to be built on Morris Island. It has been around since 1876.
- The lighthouse has endured earthquakes, hurricanes, neglect, and erosion.

Morris Island Lighthouse, about 1900, showing the keeper's house and equipment shed, as well as a retaining wall.

lighthouse was designed to be like the lighthouses at the Outer Banks of North Carolina. It was painted with the same black and white horizontal striping pattern as Bodie Island Lighthouse.

Windows are at different levels on the east and west sides of the lighthouse. Nine stories of steps lead up to the lantern room. The lighting system included a first-order Fresnel lens.

The lighthouse keeper and his two assistants lived in the three-story keeper's house with their families. There were fifteen buildings around the lighthouse. These included the keeper's house, a barn, sheds, and a one-room schoolhouse. The teacher was brought over by rowboat on Mondays and returned to the mainland on Fridays. The keepers kept livestock and also maintained a vegetable garden to help feed their large families.

An 1885 hurricane and an 1886 earthquake created big cracks in the lighthouse. World War II bombing practice on nearby Folly Island made these cracks much worse.

The channel leading into Charleston Harbor shifted. This meant that jetties had to be built to keep the channel open. The jetties to protect the harbor were done in 1889. The jetties were needed but they caused erosion problems for Morris Island. The erosion was bad enough that it caused damage to the foundation of the lighthouse. The lighthouse began to lean slightly.

A bad hurricane nearly destroyed the keeper's house. Island erosion got worse because of the storms. For their safety, the keepers were removed from Morris Island. The fifteen buildings on the island were also moved or destroyed. The lighthouse was automated that same year. The first-order Fresnel lens was removed. Acetylene (a flammable gas) was used to light the automated lamp. Sullivan's Island Lighthouse was built in 1962. The old Morris Island Lighthouse was no longer needed. The government sold Morris Island Lighthouse to a private citizen. In 1999, a nonprofit group, Save the Light, bought the lighthouse for $75,000. Ownership was transferred to the government of South Carolina. It is leased to Save the Light for ninety-nine years. This group is responsible for the care and repairs of this historic lighthouse. Save the Light has begun repairing the lighthouse. It will be a long and costly process. It remains to be seen if the group will be able to save this old beacon.

Cool Stuff to Do

Take a fun cruise around Charleston Harbor. You'll see lots of sights, including Fort Sumter. There are also tours of the fort. Visitors can hear about what it was like for the soldiers who served there. They wore wool uniforms even in August! After your harbor cruise, don't miss Patriots Point Naval Museum. Patriots Point is the world's largest naval and maritime museum. On display are the World War II aircraft carrier USS *Yorktown*, the destroyer USS *Laffey*, submarines, Coast Guard cutters, and much more.

Hunting Island Lighthouse

This lighthouse was needed to guide ships from Charleston and Beaufort to Savannah. It was decided that two lighthouses were needed here. The main lighthouse would be a cone-shaped brick tower built topped with a brass lantern second-order Fresnel lens. The light would flash every thirty seconds and be seen seventeen miles away. The smaller lighthouse would be a thirty-two-foot-high wooden lighthouse. It would have a nonblinking sixth-order Fresnel lens. There are no records indicating that the second beacon was ever built.

The Hunting Island Light Station was built in 1859. It was destroyed during the Civil War. Another lighthouse was built closer to the shore. It cost $102,000. Cast-iron plates weighing 1,200 pounds each were used to build the tower. The plates were numbered so that workers knew where to put each piece. The lighthouse was made this way in case it had to be moved. Erosion was a big problem on Hunting Island so it was expected that the lighthouse would have to be moved sometime.

Construction was delayed by crew illness. Many came down with malaria. This was caused by mosquito bites. The 136-foot-tall lighthouse was finished in 1875. Its light came from a 100,000-candlepower beam. It flashed every thirty seconds. The lamp was lit by kerosene. The light was reflected through a second-order Fresnel lens.

A three-story keepers' house was built. It had twelve rooms. They were all needed for the keeper, his two assistants, and their families. An

oil shed and two storage buildings were built nearby.

In 1889, the lighthouse had to be taken apart and moved a little over a mile south. The tower was put back together and relit on October 1, 1889. If you visit, look closely and you can see the numbers on the iron plates that builders used to rebuild the tower. The lighthouse was shut down on June 16, 1933.

It is the only lighthouse in South Carolina open to the public. Visitors can climb 176 steps to the top. The oil shed is now a small museum. It shows the history of the lighthouse.

FUN FACTS

- Hunting Island Lighthouse is made up of cast-iron plates. It was designed so that it could be taken apart, moved, and put back together in another location (like a puzzle).
- The lighthouse is located inside the five-thousand-acre Hunting Island State Park.
- Hunting Island Lighthouse is the only lighthouse in the state open to the public.

BUILDING A LIGHTHOUSE WAS NO SMALL JOB.

It was done by manual labor. Building supplies often had to be brought by boat. A path through the overgrowth had to be cleared from the boat dock to where the lighthouse was being built. It took months or years to build a lighthouse. Bad weather, war, location, and not enough money often got in the way of construction.

Supplies for lighthouse construction were brought in by horse-drawn wagon.

Hunting Island Lighthouse

Hilton Head Lighthouse

The Hilton Head Lighthouse is often called the Rear Range Lighthouse because it was once the rear light of two towers whose lights were lined up to guide ships into the channel.

A group of men from the West Indies sent an English explorer to this island in 1664. Hilton Head Island was named in honor of this explorer, William Hilton.

A small tower to guide ships was built during the Civil War by Union soldiers. It was destroyed by a storm six years later.

After the war, the government gave $40,000 for a lighthouse project. It was used to buy land and put two range lights on Hilton Head Island. The lights were lit in 1881.

The front light was a thirty-five-foot tower on top of the keeper's house. The rear light was a ninety-four-foot tower a mile away from the front light. The front light was flashing. The rear light was fixed. The two lights had to line up perfectly. One had to be exactly above the other one. This is how sea captains would know how to enter the channel. In 1884, the front beacon had to be changed so that it could be moved because the channel had shifted over time.

Both the front and rear lights needed to be moveable or they wouldn't line up perfectly.

There were two keepers' houses, a boathouse, a small wharf, and

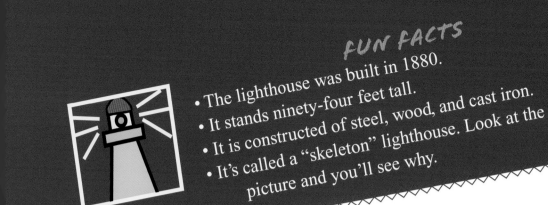

several outbuildings. They have been destroyed by storms. The only buildings that have survived are the rear light, the main keeper's house, and a brick oil shed. The keeper's house was sold and moved to another part of the island.

The rear light is sometimes called the Rear Range Lighthouse of Hilton Head. Nowadays, it is just known as the Hilton Head Lighthouse. The tower is made of steel and cast iron. The watch room and lantern room were made of cypress wood. The wood was later replaced with steel. Six large concrete foundation pilings anchor the lighthouse. One is in the middle of the tower. It was put there to support its 112-step circular metal staircase. The keeper had to go out to the oil shed to get the kerosene. He carried the kerosene up the staircase several times a night. He climbed the stairs again the following morning to put the lamp out. His days were spent cleaning the lighting system and trimming its wick. He also washed the lantern room windows.

The tower sits on Palmetto Dunes Resort's golf course. The course was designed so that the lighthouse wouldn't have to be torn down.

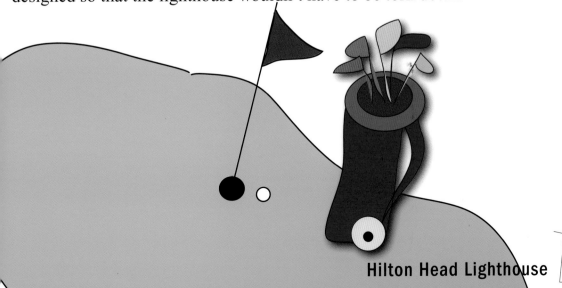

Hilton Head Lighthouse

Harbour Town "Lighthouse"

Harbour Town Lighthouse was the last lighthouse built in South Carolina. It is privately owned by Sea Pines Plantation. It cost $68,000 to build in 1969. The lighthouse is six-sided to help protect it from salt water and corrosion.

The little red-and-white-striped beacon stands ninety feet tall. It has 110 steps to the top. The light flashes every two and a half seconds from a low-watt bulb. It can be seen fifteen miles away on a clear night. Visitors are permitted to climb the lighthouse for a view of the marina. This lighthouse is listed on Coast Guard maps but is really nothing more than a daymark or landmark. It is not considered by most lighthouse enthusiasts to be a real lighthouse.

Haig Point Lighthouses

Haig Point Rear Lighthouse

Daufuskie Island in 1873. Two were needed because they were range lights, not lighthouses. There are front and rear range lights. Usually, the rear light is on top of the keeper's house. The front light is a little beacon that can be moved. The Haig Point range lights were needed to guide ships into Savannah and Charleston. They were named in honor of a Daufuskie Island plantation owner, George Haig.

The two lights were a half mile from each another. The rear light was on the keeper's house. It had a fixed white light and a fifth-order Fresnel lens.

The front beacon was also made of wood. It didn't have a Fresnel lens. It had a steamer lens. These lenses were made for steam engine locomotives but found to be useful in some light towers. The lights at Haig Point were shut off in July 1924.

The rear light is still listed on Coast Guard maps as a daymark. You have to climb stairs and ladders to reach the lantern room. There is a 247-candlepower beam inside a large acrylic optic lens. It is powered by a solar battery. It flashes for two seconds every ten seconds.

There were also two range lights on the south tip of Daufuskie Island. The Bloody Point range lights were nearly the same as those at Haig Point. The lantern room on top of the keeper's house was removed when the lights were no longer needed.

Haig Point Front Lighthouse

FUN FACTS

- Haig Point Lighthouses sat abandoned for many years. It was restored in the 1980s.
- The first Haig Point lighthouse keeper was Patrick Comer. He made $560 a year. His wife, Bridget, was assistant keeper. Her salary was $400 a year.
- A Bloody Point lighthouse keeper converted the oil house into a winery in the 1950s. Arthur "Papy" Burns used island fruit to make wine for himself and his friends!

Lighthouse Quiz

The answers to all these questions can be found throughout this book. Try to find the answers in the book before you look at the next section.

1. What is the first known lighthouse built in the world?

2. What was the first lighthouse built in America?

3. How many lighthouses were in America at the end of the Revolutionary War?

4. What is the only lighthouse in South Carolina that has air conditioning?

5. What is the tallest lighthouse in America?

6. What is a "wickie?"

7. Lighthouse keepers made lots of money. True or false?

8. Who is responsible for our lighthouses today?

9. What was the purpose of a lightship?

10. Were there lightships in the Carolinas?

11. Were there any female lighthouse keepers?

12. Who was the last keeper at Cape Hatteras Lighthouse?

13. What North Carolina Island was known as a pirates' haven?

14. Cabbage was used to make oil to light the beacons. True or false?

15. Name an octagonal lighthouse. Hint: This means eight-sided.

16. What kind of lighthouse is Harbour Town?

17. Where are the last two Texas-style light towers located in the Carolinas?

18. Name three materials that were used to build a lighthouse.

19. Where is the only skeletal lighthouse in the Carolinas?

20. The twin tower rule says that when a new lighthouse is built, the old one must be destroyed. This is so the old tower won't become a danger or confuse ships. What is the exception to this rule? Hint: It's in South Carolina.

Lighthouse Quiz Answers

(Note: The answers to all these questions can be found throughout this book. Try to find the answers for yourself).

**(FYI stands for "For Your Information."
The FYIs here give you a little more information about the topic.)**

1. Pharos Lighthouse. It was built in 280 B.C.
FYI: The oldest surviving lighthouse is La Coruna in Spain. It dates back to 20 B.C.

2. Boston Light. It was built in 1716.
FYI: The oldest surviving lighthouse in America is Sandy Hook Lighthouse in New Jersey. It dates back to 1764 and is still in use. Though the Boston Light is the first because the original was built in 1716, it was destroyed and the second Boston Light wasn't built until 1783.

3. There were twelve lighthouses in America in 1783.

4. Sullivan's Island Lighthouse is one of the last beacons built in our country. Because it has offices in the base of the tower, air conditioning was put in to keep the workers cool during the hot summer months.

5. Cape Hatteras Lighthouse: 197 feet.
FYI: Some sources say the lighthouse is 207 feet tall, but ten of those feet are underground, so they don't really count!

6. This was the nickname given to lighthouse keepers because they used to have to trim the lamp wicks every day so that the light worked properly.

7. False. Being a lighthouse keeper was an important job, but it didn't pay well. Some keepers had to take second jobs or grow food and raise farm animals to feed their families.

8. Records indicate around 1,500 lighthouses have been built in America. Some states, such as Michigan and Maine, had close to one hundred at one time.

9. Lightships were used when a lighthouse couldn't be built. These ships had lights at the top of their masts and most had fog bells.

10. Yes. North Carolina had several over the years, including Diamond Shoals Lightship and Frying Pan Shoals Lightship.

11. There were female lighthouse keepers, but most weren't hired. They took over the job when a father or husband, who was the official keeper, became ill or died. Records indicate there have been 80 female keepers.

12. "Cap'n" Unaka Jennette was the last keeper at Cape Hatteras Lighthouse. He was the keeper from 1919 to 1939. He lived there with his wife, "Miss Sudie," and their seven children.

13. Ocracoke Island.

14. True. At one time, cabbages were squeezed and the liquid was used to make oil. It was called Coiza oil.
FYI: Lard oil (animal fat made into oil) was also used! So was whale oil!

15. Bald Head Island

16. This is not considered to be a real lighthouse. The six-sided tower is a landmark for Sea Pines Plantation Marina.

17. They are in the water! Frying Pan Shoals Light Tower is at Frying Pan Shoals (Cape Fear) and Diamond Shoals Light Tower is at Diamond Shoals (Hatteras Island).

18. Concrete, brick, steel, stone, wood, cast-iron, and tabby.

19. Hilton Head Lighthouse

20. Cape Romain Lighthouses

Photo Credits

TZ – Terrance Zepke
NCSA – North Carolina State Archives
NA – National Archives
OBHC – Outer Banks History Center
DCTB – Dare County Tourist Bureau
NCTT – North Carolina Travel and Tourism
SM – Image courtesy of Sarah McNeil
BCT – Brunswick County Tourism
MC – Martin Coble
IPRC – International Paper Realty Corp.
MS – Illustration by Michael Swing
LH – Lighthouse
JR – Illustration by Julie Rabun

Title page – TZ **p.2** – Currituck LH, TZ; Cape Lookout LH, NCTT; Georgetown LH, MC **p. 4** – Pharos LH, MS **p. 6** – Boston Light, MS **p. 9** – MS **p. 11** – NCSA **p. 13** – MS **p. 18** – TZ **p. 19** – TZ **p. 20** – Whalehead Club, NCSA; lighthouse keepers and families posing at Currituck LH, NA **p. 21** – Bodie Island LH, TZ **p. 22** – Bodie Island LH stairs, OBHC; Wright brothers monument, TZ **p. 23** – TZ **p. 24** – Bill Garrett, North Carolina Division of Archives and History **p. 26** – Dog in boat, MS; Cape Hatteras Life-Saving Station, NCSA **p. 27** – Ocracoke LH, DCTB **p. 28** – aerial view of Ocracoke Island, DCTB; Blackbeard photo, NCSA **p. 29** – NCTT **p. 30** – Cape Lookout LH, NCSA; wild pony, North Carolina division of Tourism, Film and Sports Development **p. 31** – NCTT **p. 32** – ladder to lantern room, TZ; helicopters placing lamp, NCSA **p. 33** – Price Creek LH, NCSA; "The Old Lighthouse," NCSA **p. 34** – TZ **p. 35** – SM **p. 36** – Diamond Shoals Light Tower, circa 1980, NCSA **p. 37** – Frying Pan Light Tower, circa 1980, NCSA; Frying Pan Shoals Lightship, NCSA **p. 40** – Georgetown LH, MC; Georgetown LH with keepers' house, 22 April 1893, NA **p. 42** – JR **p. 43** – TZ **p. 44** – NA **p. 45** – JR **p. 46** – TZ **p. 47** – TZ **p. 48** – TZ **p. 49** – NA **p. 51** – TZ **p. 52** – TZ **p. 53** – MS **p. 54** – Hilton Head LH and oil shed, TZ; close-up of Hilton Head LH, TZ **p. 56** – TZ **p. 57** – Haig Point Rear LH, 1994, IPRC **p. 58** – Haig Point Front LH, 11 June 1885, NA

Index